YoungWriters

WONDER VERSE

A Creative Wonderland

Edited By Wendy Laws

First published in Great Britain in 2025 by:

YoungWriters
— Est. 1991 —

Young Writers
Remus House
Coltsfoot Drive
Peterborough
PE2 9BF
Telephone: 01733 890066
Website: www.youngwriters.co.uk

FOREWORD

WELCOME READER,

For Young Writers' latest competition *Wonderverse*, we asked primary school pupils to explore their creativity and write a poem on any topic that inspired them. They rose to the challenge magnificently with some going even further and writing stories too! The result is this fantastic collection of writing in a variety of styles.

Here at Young Writers our aim is to encourage creativity in children and to inspire a love of the written word, so it's great to get such an amazing response, with some absolutely fantastic pieces. This open theme of this competition allowed them to write freely about something they are interested in, which we know helps to engage kids and get them writing. Within these pages you'll find a variety of topics, from hopes, fears and dreams, to favourite things and worlds of imagination. The result is a collection of brilliant writing that showcases the creativity and writing ability of the next generation.

I'd like to congratulate all the young writers in this anthology, I hope this inspires them to continue with their creative writing.

CONTENTS

Ada Cakirer (8) 62
Noar Xhigoli (8) 63
Alex Tun (8) 64
Sami Christofi (9) 65
Ava-Rose Townsend (9) 66
Ariadni Tsalia (8) 67
Raphael Sokhal (8) 68
Daria Tajbakhsh-Malysko (8) 69
Sophie Smith (9) 70
Katerina Frantzanas (8) 71
Hasan Akarcay-Gungor (8) 72
Abtin Abtin (8) 73
Meryem Mercan (8) 74
Luca Murray (9) 75
Aria Jangra (8) & Alexis 76
Zachary Osijo (8) 77
Malak Mahran (8) 78
Rian Mistry (8) 79
Selim Suleyman (8) 80
Zaida Hazzan (9) 81
Ava Parsons (8) 82
Oliver Kola (8) 83
Nazanin Farhadi (8) 84
Jasmine Shevket (8) 85
Sayna Mofrad (8) 86
Libbie Angelides (9) 87
Dimitri Karasas (9) 88
Ebrah Ali (9) 89
Vincent Palmer (8) 90
Aaron Doondeea (8) 91
Alphan Selim Sener (9) 92
Kristian Koceku (8) 93
Leo Kyriacou (8) 94
Rory Megahey Townend (8) 95
Atlas Ulgu (9) 96
Lyra Codling (8) 97
Lilly Desai (8) 98
Siyena Erboy (8) 99
Wynter Reyes (8) 100
Ruby Rogers (8) 101
Hektor Kukeli (9) & Rafael 102
Refahi (8)

Lisnasharragh Primary School, Cregagh

Tom Scott (11) 103
Kale Holland (11) 104

Seabridge Primary School, Clayton

Emily Morbey (8) 105
Orlaith Rogers (9) 106
Niamh Rogers (8) 108
Emily Leech (9) 110
Pollyanna Rushton (8) 112
Cara O'Neill (8) 114
Ananya Manjunatha (8) 116
Charlie Allen (8) 117
Hashim Riaz (8) 118
Ryan Kumar (8) 119
Esme Twigg (8) 120
Zachary Hopwood (9) 121
Ben Lowery (8) 122
Leo Saunders (8) 123
Benjamin Willday (9) 124
Oliver Taylor (8) 125
Lincoln Messenger (8) 126
Nia Koshy (8) 127
Theo Roe-Griffiths (8) 128
David Kuruvilla (8) 129
Oliver Heath (9) 130
Risu Kumar (8) 131
Ethan Cole (8) 132
Flick Taylor (8) 133
Ronnie Abercrombie (8) 134
Alfie Richards (8) 135
Ahmad Ali (8) 136
James Raby (8) 137
Henry Vincent (8) 138
Lucas Peart (9) 139
Max Bailey (8) 140
Lucas Raby (8) 141
Aryan Cheema (9) 142
Annabelle Davies (8) 143
George Jones (9) 144

Raghavi Kohileanthiran (8)	145
Feyza Kose (8)	146
Wyatt Roberts (8)	147
Olivia Leech (8)	148
Annabel Johnson (8)	149
Jude Mellenchip (8)	150
Alfie Dalgarno (8)	151
Alessi Collis (8)	152
Tyler Mclean (8)	153
Raees Mahmood (8)	154
Florence Green (8)	155

St Peter's Primary School, Bromyard

Ayanna Kirsop-Moran (10)	156
Emilia Jordan (11)	159
Mason Baker (10)	160
Delna Siby (11)	162
Indie Mills (10)	164
Poppy Eversham (11)	166
Joshua Nhemwa (11)	168
Ellie Evans (10)	170
Danella Major (10)	172
Olivia Mae (10)	173
Bethany Cross (10)	174
Edie Meddins (11)	176
Phoebe Phillips (10)	177
Alex Oakley (10)	178
Rebekah Perfect (10)	180
Albie Cartwright (10)	181
Julia Jaromin (10)	182
Theo Brittain (10)	183
Isabel Bilyard (11)	184
Benjamin Taylor (10)	185
Olivia-Rose Weaver (11)	186
Lucas Harper (10)	187
Jessica Maine (10)	188
Amber Backhouse (10)	189
Esmae Greaves (10)	190
Noel Marchant (10)	191
Isabella Pilliner (10)	192
Bright Mupedzi (11)	193
Abhia Abhilash (10)	194

Abigail Sabau (10)	195

St Theresa's Catholic Primary School, Blacon

Tilly Denton (10)	196
Daisy Andrews (9)	198
Syra Howell (10)	199
Daisy Partington (9)	200
Araoluwa Ijasan (9)	201
Rita Hughes (9)	202
Crimson Harris (10)	203
Kaiden Hampshire (9)	204
Alain Kamtchouang (9)	205
Jacob Andrews (9)	206
Poppy Barnett (9)	207
Cara Connally (10)	208
Jeffery Ogedegbe (9)	209
Jake Mapp (9)	210

THE CREATIVE WRITING

In The Realm Of Imagination

In the Realm of Imagination, anything is possible
You can see anything simply by imagining
You could see pixies, dragons or anything

In the Realm of Imagination, anything is possible
You can smell anything simply by imagining
You could smell mystical flowers, golden cookies or anything

In the Realm of Imagination, anything is possible
You can hear anything simply by imagining
You could hear a dragon roaring, a twig snapping or anything

In the Realm of Imagination, anything is possible
You can feel anything simply by imagining
You could feel soft grass, the harsh cold sea or anything

In the Realm of Imagination, anything is possible
You can taste anything simply by imagining
You could taste salty water, cooked fish or anything

Even though the way to this realm is hidden
Like the story to this poem, you can find it easily.

Bluebell Dovey (10)
Cliddesden Primary School, Cliddesden

Climate Change

The world is changing, beware,
Is it only me who is aware?

Deforestation
The Amazon rainforest and plenty of others are getting
destroyed,
Oxygen trying to be free, swaying in the air filling our
lungs but the oxygen is depositing,
I can hear the screech of trees' boughs.

The world is changing, beware,
Is it only me who is aware?

The underwater sea
Sea turtles suffocating, barnacles sticking to their
backs pulling them down in the depths,
Turtles live on the line caught!

The world is changing, beware,
Is it only me who is aware?

Poachers
Stealing their lives, no love in their hearts except plenty
for money.

Taking their tusks and chopping them down, they kill
elephants and rhinos leaving an unfillable amount.
I can feel the revolting sting of animals dying.

The world is changing, beware,
Is it only me who is aware?

The red trauma
Falling numbers, danger everywhere, the red squirrel's
cousin, the greys, are sending them into extinction.

The world is changing, beware,
Is it only *me* who is aware?
It is time to change!

Silvie Rogers (10)
Cliddesden Primary School, Cliddesden

I Didn't...

I didn't score the game-winning goal in the Stanley Cup final,
But I did play ice hockey in my garden.
I didn't go to Paris to watch the Olympics,
But I did stream it on my TV.
I didn't drive a Lamborghini in Monaco,
But I did drive a toy car at my house.
I didn't watch Leonardo da Vinci draw the Mona Lisa,
But I did watch my sister draw a replica.
I didn't witness a mass shooting where somebody died,
But I did see my sister get hit in the eye with a Nerf gun,
Possibly the most painful thing known to mankind.
I didn't score a three-pointer in the NBA.
Now watch as I screw this piece of paper up
And throw it into the bin from the other side of the classroom.
Just another piece of paper full of countless ideas to add to the bin's collection.

James Chandler (10)
Cliddesden Primary School, Cliddesden

I Didn't...

I didn't feel the spray of Niagara Falls,
But I did watch the rain drizzle down my window.
I didn't go to a five-star gourmet restaurant,
But I did go to a pretend cafe in my garden.

I didn't go drinking in a bar,
But I did drink a glass of water.
I didn't relax in a luxury limousine,
But I did go around the garden in a toy car.

I didn't fight zombies in the abyss of the Earth,
But I did play-fight with an imaginary friend.
I didn't score the winning shot in the championship finals,
But I did throw a tennis ball into an umbrella.

But watch this piece of paper get torn up and thrown into the depths of the bin.
Never to be seen again.
Along with many other great ideas that never ventured further than these four walls.

Joseph Ball (10)
Cliddesden Primary School, Cliddesden

All Emotions Are Okay

Emotions such as happiness,
Emotions such as sadness,
All emotions are okay and none of them are bad.

Sometimes you feel a little bit sad,
Sometimes you feel a little bit hurt,
But they're all okay,
We feel them every day.

Sometimes we feel calm,
Sometimes we feel proud,
But they're all fine,
They all shine.

Sometimes we feel silly,
Sometimes we feel confused,
But they all fuse,
They're in you.

Sometimes we feel panicked and that's okay too,
Sometimes we feel like we need to step out of the room,
But they're all okay,
We feel them every day.

Emma Gallagher (9)
Cliddesden Primary School, Cliddesden

The Darkness In Wonderverse

Sharp winds shot past her like a gun
Never-ending tears poured down her face
An icy cold breeze blew continuously

Grey birds landed on her like she was a dead tree
Dust flew around like a flock of pigeons
Silence fell over the forest like a blanket

Cobwebs flew in the gritty air
Lightning struck like a knife
Dark clouds hovered like flies

Darkness spread over Wonderverse as the sun set.

Elsie London (10)
Cliddesden Primary School, Cliddesden

Autumn

When the sun won't shine so brightly
And the leaves start to fall
People start to wear warmer clothes
I like to snuggle in a blanket too
Put up a movie on the TV with some hot cocoa on
the side
Autumn's the best season, obviously
Just wait for the rain to subside
When the ground is covered with brown and gold
Some people go inside
But most stay out and play in the leaf piles.

Zoe Cornish (9)
Cliddesden Primary School, Cliddesden

The Spirits Of The Light

Gleaming and glowing
A small spark comes alive
Breaking through the dark
It sparkles and dazzles

Stars start to show
Nature starts to grow
Vines grow out like a blessing
The world starts to brighten up

The stars start to dance with joy
Spirits start to light up the world
Jumping around being the brightest of them all
Giving the world its true colours.

Caitlin Busby (10)
Cliddesden Primary School, Cliddesden

The Monster

A fearsome creature
With ugly feathers,
It has yellow fur
And a long grey nose,
So always be aware.

Its smell is bad,
It smells like rotten fish,
But don't be fooled,
It's still a fearsome creature,
So always be aware.

Its roar is brutal,
As loud as motorways,
So before you move,
You won't hear anything,
So always be aware.

Roo Nunn (9)
Cliddesden Primary School, Cliddesden

Dumb Dodo

D ecisions that we have made
O f our hunger
D odo bird is led to extinction
O ught we do to unextinct this bird?

B ut even with all our technology
I t shall stay extinct as its curiosity decided its fate
R eliving this time, would we have chosen differently?
D odo's eyes will never see the light of day again.

Louisa Hastings (10)
Cliddesden Primary School, Cliddesden

The Odd And Super Banana!

There was a super banana
Which could jump into space and back.
This time he got stuck in space.
You would think that he would die from lack of oxygen.
You would be wrong - it's a banana,
Not an animal or human, a banana.

Finally, I'm awake.
That was a crazy dream!

Zak Anthony (9)
Cliddesden Primary School, Cliddesden

Horses

Some are big, some are small,
Some are wide, some are tall,
Some are feisty, some are calm,
Some hate being in a barn,
Some are loud, some are quiet,
Some are always in a riot,
Some are just annoyingly cool,
And some like playing with a ball.

Charlotte Jordan (10)
Cliddesden Primary School, Cliddesden

Football

F un to play football
O ccasionally score a goal
O ften win games
T ry your best
B aller means skilful
A ctivation is key in football
L earn to score
L earn to play.

Kian Donnelly (10)
Cliddesden Primary School, Cliddesden

Football

F un to play
G **O** od skills
G **O** od shots
T eamwork
B eing amazing
A nd there's a goalkeeper
L ook - a ball
L et's go and play.

Teddy Dale (9)
Cliddesden Primary School, Cliddesden

The Penguin

Black flipper,
Power swimmer,
Warmth huddler,
Fish hunter,
Strong chewer,
Fast tobogganer,
Breath holder.
Flightless flier.

Hugo Roberts (10)
Cliddesden Primary School, Cliddesden

Blue Tit

A haiku

Gliding to the trees,
You numb the anxiety,
Fly up to the clouds.

Raymon Morrison (10)
Cliddesden Primary School, Cliddesden

Prisoner

I was kept in a cage,
Filled with my own rage
I had done nothing wrong
Yet for forgiveness and happiness I long

But it's too late
For I am here for the rest of my life
I won't ever leave through that gate
Where I can flee and strife

I was stabbed in the back
By my own best friend
There is something that I lack
After all, best friend has an end

Never, has an ever
Friend, has an end,
I guess nothing lasts forever
This is it, the end.

Tamyia Skelsey (12)
Dane Court Grammar School, Broadstairs

The Dragon's Lair

The dragon's lair whispers in the air,
Taking away our happiness,
Switching it with despair.

As you enter the medieval castle,
The floor screeches and hisses,
You tremble in the dim, dark hallway,
The thick, grey smoke spirals around your body,
The brown bricks reach out to space,
As the door creaks open,
What could it be?

Our eyes open as wide as the sun
Oh, we're not here to have fun.

As your eyes adjust,
A colossal creature emerges from the smoke,
Green scales shimmer in the shadowy distance.

Its red eyes fiercely glow
Its cape flawlessly bounces in the wind
Its nostrils are packed with smoke.

Don't go on,
Beware...
Because it's coming for you!

Sophia Brennan (9)
Grange Park Primary School, Winchmore Hill

Christmas At School

On the morning of Christmas, Santa jumps into his sleigh, with one town in his mind...
The London Borough of Enfield, it's small but it's so bright! So off he goes to every school,
delivering presents to the children at the school hall!
All the children are waiting for Santa to visit their home, but little did they know that they were never ever alone!
Santa first delivers to Grange Park Primary School, then Eversley, after Merryhills School too.
Next in line is Enfield Town so even the grown-ups here, don't need to frown.
So all the children, big and small, celebrate Christmas but this time in school!

Merry Christmas to you all!

Alexander Mario (8)
Grange Park Primary School, Winchmore Hill

The Environment

E arth is a place where we all live.

N ature made this beautiful world of ours.

V igilant people will care for the world.

I n the modern world, simple things can help.

R ecycle and reuse as much as you can.

O ther people take care of the planet like it is their baby.

N o other planet where life can begin.

M arvellous place should look like paradise.

E verybody should take care of our Earth as big as the galaxy.

N obody should litter with disgusting rubbish.

T he twisted trees sway slowly in the wind.

Sienna Shah (8)
Grange Park Primary School, Winchmore Hill

The Secret Garden

You can see a rainbow ending at the end of the big garden,
You can see the insects flying around the mysterious garden.

You can hear bees flying around the garden making honey in their nests,
You can hear the flowers dancing in the cold winter breeze.

You can smell the red beautiful roses smelling like candyfloss,
You can smell the green beautiful trees looking after the big mysterious garden.

You can feel the squirrels running around the tall big trees looking for some food,
You can feel the leaves twirling around their beautiful branches joyfully.

Nehir Sepetci (8)
Grange Park Primary School, Winchmore Hill

Turtle Ranger

T urtle Ranger powers through the deep blue sea,
U nderwater he can see tiny terrapins swimming free.
R ushing through the enormous ocean,
T iger sharks making a commotion.
L arge starfish playing on the sea floor,
E very day he goes and explores.

R unning to help the sea horses,
A nd untangling them with his strong forces.
N ever letting any animal suffer,
G oing to help a stranded puffer.
E very sea creature is safe and sound,
R ushing home he starts to pound.

Henry Bell (9)
Grange Park Primary School, Winchmore Hill

Healthy Environment

E arth is a place where we all live

N ature has so many gifts to give

V ast trees that sway around in the windy wind

I n the modern world, simple things will help

R ecycle and reuse as much as you can

O ur world should be a safe place to live in

N o other planet where life can begin

M arvellous place like paradise our world can be

E veryone should understand this

N ever forget that our planet's wealth

T he environment is as important as your health.

Emily Tudzharova (9)

Grange Park Primary School, Winchmore Hill

Halloween

H alloween night, kids want to go trick or treating.

A loud knock at the door, it was a friend shrouded.

L oudly, Halloween, we were jumping happily.

L oud bang hit the ground but we ignored it.

"O h no," someone shouted, we checked, no one was there.

W e just skipped around trick or treating all around.

E nergetic children running across the street to get some sweets.

E lephant chocolate getting handed out, children are running around.

N ever ever miss Halloween.

Scarlett Petrou (8)
Grange Park Primary School, Winchmore Hill

The Haunted Shadow

Let's go to a haunted school,
There a legend will tell a mythical story,
About a shadow that whispered and screeched all
night,
Through a dark gloomy corridor,
A shadow that goes bang and crash through the night,
But there still lurks a shapeshifting mythical creature.

But in the principal's office,
Lurk other legendary creatures,
That wake up in the night,
And do haunted spooky things,
Through the day they go to haunted spooky
graveyards,
They spook people and haunt them through the night.

Louis Cruse (9)
Grange Park Primary School, Winchmore Hill

My Idol

Let's meet him,
He is inspiring and exciting,
He is nice and can be naughty,
He is fun but never boring,
He has a tiny ego but I still love my uncle.

His name is the spectacular Aaron Lennon,
He makes my family cheer,
Boom! He scores again, he is a shining star,
I love who you are.
He is as fast as a leopard,
And has met many legends.

We know him for his talent and ability,
10 years at the club,
And as happy as a cub.
I love you,
And you are my idol.

Josh Young (9)
Grange Park Primary School, Winchmore Hill

Pluto

Let's go to Pluto,
Pluto is a blue bouncy planet that is as spectacular
as the fireworks on New Year's Eve,
I can hear a whistle sound coming from Pluto,
I can smell a bonfire coming from Pluto,
I can hear banging coming from Pluto.

Pluto is as vibrant as a rainbow emerging from the
clouds,
Pluto is as hot as sand sizzling in the sun,
Around Pluto, it is as dark as the night sky.

Pluto is a dangerous, gloomy planet,
Pluto is blue and true,
Pluto is small and cool.

Dylan Golding (8)
Grange Park Primary School, Winchmore Hill

Halloween

H is for Halloween during which you can go out and have memories,

A is for the awesome time you have,

L is for the gentle leaves that pile up in a bunch,

L is for the light guiding your way,

O is for all the old houses you get candy from,

W is for the wind that blows in your face,

E is for all the enormous sweets or chocolate bars you get,

E is for all the elephant costumes,

N is for all the mums saying, "No more sweets!"

Albert Parish (9)

Grange Park Primary School, Winchmore Hill

Mother Nature

Mother Nature's glory
And her simple stories
My granny used to tell
By the river well,
From a great old seashell,
The leaves all quickly fell.

My granny said I needed to explain,
I was wisely walking down a lane.
A long time ago I saw leaves,
Falling alone and I said, "Mother Nature, Mother Nature."
All the leaves fell and said, "You're welcome."
Same with the trees, branches and wood, they all Whispered, "You're welcome."

Alexia Liasedis (9)
Grange Park Primary School, Winchmore Hill

Bertie – My Pet Dog

This is my pet, Bertie,
Whenever he's bored, we take him to the park,
And that's when he has a little bark,
Sometimes he steals my food,
Which gets me in a bad mood,
Sometimes he gets in a bit of trouble,
But he likes to play in a puddle,
This is my dog,
And he likes to play in the fog.

At night, he barks as loud as a wolf,
At night, he sleeps as quietly as the moon,
At night, he settles as easily as the sea,
He comes in my room and he looks out for me.

Isabella Hall (9)
Grange Park Primary School, Winchmore Hill

Animals

In the Forbidden Forest,
Animals lurk in the shadows,
Waiting for their prey,
As the sun rises, bats return to their gloomy cave and
call it a day.

Rustling through the trees,
Heroic leopards roar,
In the sky above,
Colourful parrots soar,

While the animals heedlessly drink from the swamp,
Unaware, of what the murky waters hide,

As the moon awakes from its slumber,
The bats emerge from their dark cave,

To a forest silent and still.

Khawla Osman (9)
Grange Park Primary School, Winchmore Hill

Halloween

H orrifying Halloween as dim as a bat's cave

A terrifying party is held everywhere

L ights go out and candles go boom

L onely lands with lots of creepy vampires

O h no, time to make people jump out of their skin

W e do trick or treating to put people in delight

E xtraordinary haunted house as spooky as a ghost in fright

E merald decorations in spiky pumpkins

N ever-ending pathway with foggy roads.

Adora Euphrates (9)

Grange Park Primary School, Winchmore Hill

Space

The sun is in the sky hot and bright; it gives us light,
The beaming sun is as bright as a golden twinkling sea,
The round sun is in charge of the planets going around him.

Blazing stars are like heavy fires,
The bright shiny stars are shining in the black velvet sky,
The golden stars travel through the pitch-black sky.

If I was on a zooming rocketship, I would land on the moon,
If I was on a zooming rocket, I would steal the stars from the sky.

Pani Kassapi
Grange Park Primary School, Winchmore Hill

Countries And Continents

Continents as large as the sun,
Countries, there are a ton.
7 continents, I can't believe,
197 countries, they will achieve.

Antarctica, as cold as Mars,
Great Britain, made of chocolate bars.
Africa has the Nile, the longest river,
Canada will make you shiver.

Oceania, full of islands,
Asia has the largest country but also has Thailand.
Europe has Italy, Cyprus, UK and Greece,
North America has lots of geese.

Valentino Ioannou (9)
Grange Park Primary School, Winchmore Hill

Ninja Turtle

In the deep shadow, where silence reigns,
A ninja turtle strong, remains.
With nunchucks, swords and mighty shell,
He guards the night fights so well.
Beneath the moon, through streets he slides,
Swift as the wind, from foes he hides.
With brothers brave side by side,
Together, they'll protect with pride.
In every kick, in every strike a hero's heart, forever
bright.
A ninja path so true and bold, a truth tale of courage
told.

Olivier Lleshi (8)
Grange Park Primary School, Winchmore Hill

Guess What Sport I Am

I'm round and patterned,
And I'm a type of ball.
I'm always being kicked about,
I'm not colourful, no, not at all.
My referee always shouts and screams.
Tweet! goes the whistle,
At the end of the game.
I'm known as a hobby and sometimes an interest.
I go in the air and go on the ground,
All over the grass, you're bound to find me all around.
Have you guessed it? I am a football!

Asya Suleyman (8)
Grange Park Primary School, Winchmore Hill

Halloween

H allow's Eve, the darkest night of the year,

A night where you get treats full of fear,

L onely kids eat poisonous sweets in the

L onely, terrifying streets,

O wls come out at night,

W ith their frightening light eyes,

E ven without a bucket, you can still carry sweets,

E ven without a friend, you can still enjoy Halloween,

N o fibs, no lies, come out and try.

Milo Angelides (9)

Grange Park Primary School, Winchmore Hill

Kindness And Love

K indness is a warm hug,
I n a world of kindness, you shouldn't be sad,
N o one be sad,
D on't be bad,
N ever break things that are not yours,
E verybody be happy,
S hould we have a kind day?
S hall we be friends?

L ove lives forever,
O ur hearts full of care,
V aluable family lasts forever,
E verlasting love.

Amiya-Zuri Guishard (8)
Grange Park Primary School, Winchmore Hill

Lion Ranger

L ion Ranger lounging on a chair,
I ntelligently, he makes his way to the animal fair.
O n his way, he can see,
N aughty giraffes running free.

R unning to the large train,
A nd getting on as it rains.
N aughty monkeys everywhere,
G etting to the animal fair.
E very animal is happy now,
R elaxing while the Lion Ranger takes a bow.

Reyan Zarif (8)

Grange Park Primary School, Winchmore Hill

The Forest

Running past the mighty trees,
I can hear the buzzing bees.
Zooming past a tiny ant,
The monkeys are starting to pant.

The leaves are starting to turn red,
While the squirrels jump out of bed.
When you see a silvery trail,
You know there will be a snail.

The hunters are walking by,
Making the animals feel shy.
You can hear a crash and a bang,
And the hunters have a fang.

Nathaniel Alterman (8)
Grange Park Primary School, Winchmore Hill

My Cat

My cat has pink poofy paws as bouncy as my bouncy
blue ball,
She can bounce,
She can pounce,
She can run all around,
When I give her food,
She is in a good mood,
But when I try to cuddle her,
I get in trouble,
She has amber round eyes that glow in the gloomy
firelit night,
She adores sleeping on my pink fluffy mat,
As silent as a bat,
And as soon as she wakes up she looks for a rat.

Aleena Ali (8)
Grange Park Primary School, Winchmore Hill

Under The Sea

When I go to the sea, under the sea,
I can see dancing dolphins.

When I go to the sea, under the sea,
I can hear coral waving.

When I go to the sea, under the sea,
I can feel fish swimming around me.

When I go to the sea, under the sea,
I can smell sharks crunching fish.

When I go to the sea, under the sea,
I can taste saltwater popping on my tongue.

Fatimah Faisal (8)
Grange Park Primary School, Winchmore Hill

Space

Let's explore space,
The shimmering stars,
Meteors moving extremely fast,
The bright sun,
As round as a fresh bun.

We'll creep past the alien,
We'll fight the monsters,
We'll explore the universe.

However, we will miss home,
And our funny friends,
In the end, don't forget to rest as we snuggle up
against our father's chest.

Fred Smyth (9)
Grange Park Primary School, Winchmore Hill

Space

S hining stars in space at night but in the day the sun comes up to brighten your face,

P lanets are up there too turning like a spinning top,

A nd of course, there are aliens going whizz, bang and pop!

"C an you walk in space?" my friend asks me,

"E veryone knows you can't," I say, "there's no gravity!"

Jasmine Jarvis (8)
Grange Park Primary School, Winchmore Hill

Vampires

V icious curses lurk around the woods' shadows, screaming loudly.

A rms of grass swaying in the woods.

M agic pixies fainting with fright as it becomes a dark and gloomy night.

P athetic slug covers the path. Vampires.

I ncense of dust on the graves.

R eally, nothing is ever this scary.

E verything can be scary.

Eliza Alexander (8)

Grange Park Primary School, Winchmore Hill

It's Raining Cats And Dogs!

Dad! Dad! I went as quick as a flash,
Jumping, leaping, and I even crashed!
Bang, smash! Oh Dad, oh Dad!
It's raining cats and dogs!
Yes? Yes? Oh yes, Dad! We need an umbrella.
Bang, smash!
The cats, the dogs, meow, woof!
Phew, phew! It's stopping now.
But what about the cats and dogs?
Pest control! Oh boy, oh no!

Felicity Parkins (8)
Grange Park Primary School, Winchmore Hill

Mountains

M any people wonder how far I'll reach
O ver the rainbow I go
U nder the sea, I see the beach
N ever will I stop to wonder
T en out of ten when the dances go by
A ny more people are able to see
I n and out I go
N ever will I stop. Never will I stop
S o why can't I see you again?

Felicity Ouriach (9)
Grange Park Primary School, Winchmore Hill

Kindness

I'm just a little girl,
In this world.
Trying my best,
To beat the rest.
I try to be kind,
All the time.
Because I want everyone to be happy,
Especially the family of mine.
My heart is big,
My heart is pure,
But I want to do more.
So I hope this makes you smile,
And warms up your heart, for a little while.

Khloe Purcell (8)
Grange Park Primary School, Winchmore Hill

Nature

N ature, as beautiful as a bird gliding gracefully,
A moody monkey as lazy as a soft sofa,
T he whispering waves as calm as kittens purring,
U nkind as the dinosaurs the tigers growl,
R are as a white rhino, Komodo dragons hide from
hunters,
E ternity shall let nature thrive over the Earth.

Zachary Broom (8)

Grange Park Primary School, Winchmore Hill

Football

F ootball player kicked a ball.

O ut of the stadium.

O n a wondrous journey to a different planet.

T o somewhere magnificent Martians live.

B eyond the Martians' imagination.

A mazed but also confused.

L apping around their world.

L uminous little ball came home.

Rasitha De Zoysa (8)
Grange Park Primary School, Winchmore Hill

Football

F ootball's a great sport
O f course there are goals
O n the goals, there's a post and a bar
T hey all have different kits
B eing helpful to your teammates
A ll of the people in the crowd are chanting
L earn to have sportsmanship
L earn to shoot and pass.

Christian Leeds (8)
Grange Park Primary School, Winchmore Hill

Animals!

A mazing, awesome animals, come to me,

N othing in my path, some in the beautiful tree,

I n the bushes lurk magical creatures,

M e and you, full of sparkles,

A s we come into the light,

L ight may give you a fright,

S o see you all soon, I'm friends with the animals.

Avery Bell (8)
Grange Park Primary School, Winchmore Hill

Spring

S pring has lots of colourful and bright whistling flowers,

P erfect, pretty purple blossoms,

R ocky hills filled with multi-coloured petals,

I n spring, plants can make lots of different and delicious fruits,

N ever-ending pink, beautiful trees,

G reen grass growing up to the sky.

Sibel Saatci (8)

Grange Park Primary School, Winchmore Hill

Extinct

E ventually all animals die as slowly as a snail walking

X -rays help us know what's inside

T ap the dead animals and they won't move

I nside they have lots of disgusting blood

N o, they don't move

C ats are not extinct

T en or more animals are extinct.

Diamand Blana (8)

Grange Park Primary School, Winchmore Hill

Summer

Pretty pink flowers in tall green grass.
Fluffy little bunnies jumping past.
Spruces, willows, oaks and pines,
Leaves on branches in straight lines.
White clouds all above,
In a nest, there is a dove.
The sun shines bright, the stars are alight.
Summer is a dream with turquoise streams,
Soon summer will end and autumn will begin.

Charlotte Broom (8)
Grange Park Primary School, Winchmore Hill

Cold Summer's Day

Summer, summer is a hot day
Until a new planet came into the Milky Way,
It was cold,
Its name was Planet Cold.
Planet Cold was very, very cold.
Planet Cold was the saddest because it was as sick
as vomit.
The sun was trying to make it happy and warm.
But when he is doing that, Planet Cold cries.

Ethan Dynowski Wee (8)
Grange Park Primary School, Winchmore Hill

Summer

S un as hot as an oven,

U nder the trees, there are animals as dangerous as a bear.

M int ice cream as cold as an ice cube,

M others reminding their children to put sunscreen on them.

E merald petals shining in the sun,

R unning people shining in the summer like a diamond.

Alyssia Ketibuah (8)

Grange Park Primary School, Winchmore Hill

Nature's Side

Nature whispers, like people blowing candles for the birthday cake.
The beautiful tall trees dancing with the breeze.
Worms could smell the beautiful, fresh, colourful flowers.
The brave, beautiful butterfly was flying high like a cat trying to catch a mouse.
The colourful kingfisher is as colourful as a rainbow.

Tallulah Williams (8)
Grange Park Primary School, Winchmore Hill

Halloween Hunters

Oh no! The Halloween hunters are here to steal,
They're here for screams,
In the howling scene where no one is to be seen,

Inside the houses, they crash, they bash,
Stealing a decoration,
To get people's attention,
Souls fly up into the sky,
Ghosts are haunting each and every house.

Ayla Camp (8)
Grange Park Primary School, Winchmore Hill

Swirling Space

S tars standing tall like a holy, old chapel.

P owerful, picturesque planets skydiving high.

A mazing astronauts ready to walk on the newly discovered planets.

C osmic dust swirling and capturing my amazed eyes.

E ach planet from Earth to Mars has its own little enchanting secret.

Emilia Ollari (8)
Grange Park Primary School, Winchmore Hill

Spring Dreams

Colourful flowers were dancing
And singing with joy and exhilaration,
With a smile on their faces.
Birds were flying in the blue sky brightly.
Trees were as tall as a huge mountain.
Raindrops were dropping from the green, clear leaves.
Rabbits and robins were jumping around like frogs and kangaroos.

Ada Cakirer (8)
Grange Park Primary School, Winchmore Hill

Animals

A n anaconda is as big as a coach
N arwhals are as shiny as a mirror
I guanas are as scaly as a book
M onkeys are as cheeky as a clown
A lligators are as scary as a spider
L eopards are as spotty as a glass vase
S nakes are as venomous as a box jellyfish.

Noar Xhigoli (8)
Grange Park Primary School, Winchmore Hill

The Queen Of Birds

A little plant nice and small
Soon to grow big and tall,
The queen of birds sits on that tree
And smiles with lots of glee,
Her servants fanned her and tickled her nose,
While birds of all kinds bow at her toes,
Bzzzzz went the busy bees
As they poured her some honey lemon tea.

Alex Tun (8)

Grange Park Primary School, Winchmore Hill

Madness

M icky van de Ven
A s tall as ten children
D eadly slide tackles
N ot bad, very good
E veryone scared of him
S hot and pass as good as a spark
S uper Micky van de Ven

He's good
Not bad
He's cool
Not drool.

Sami Christofi (9)
Grange Park Primary School, Winchmore Hill

Halloween

H alloween is as fun as can be,

A s dark as space,

L ove Halloween,

L onely streets,

O range pumpkins staring at me,

W e go trick or treating,

E ating yummy sweets,

E njoying the time of our lives,

N ever steal sweets.

Ava-Rose Townsend (9)
Grange Park Primary School, Winchmore Hill

The North London Derby

The players running their best but no one is going
to rest,
Tottenham fighting for the Champions League and
Arsenal fighting for the title,
Everyone is going to be trying their hardest to get a
historic win,
But no one is going to be gentle,
Everyone is going to be tossing and tumbling.

Ariadni Tsalia (8)
Grange Park Primary School, Winchmore Hill

The Fantastic Footballer

The fantastic footballer scored high in the top bins,
The crowd went wild when he celebrated his win.
After the game when he went home,
His family was still talking about his brilliant goal.

The next day, when he woke up,
He remembered dreaming of himself winning the World Cup.

Raphael Sokhal (8)
Grange Park Primary School, Winchmore Hill

Black Cat

B ouncing over fences
L eaping into trees
A s he hunts fish
C atching birds
K nowing how to cast a fright

C alling his spooky friends
A t a speed of 100, he pounces freely
T he black cat feasts on his night meal.

Daria Tajbakhsh-Malysko (8)
Grange Park Primary School, Winchmore Hill

Pumas

P umas don't roar, all they do is purr
U nderground looking for food to eat
M aking dens to store food and keep their fur warm
A n amazing animal, strong and brave
S tarting life is hard because when they're born, they are blind in their cave.

Sophie Smith (9)

Grange Park Primary School, Winchmore Hill

Nature

Nature is shadowy and deadly sometimes
As beautiful as a shiny bush and flower
Beware, danger is here and there

Nature is beautiful like spring
Use this map and it will lead you to the woods
Read this sign; it will tell you that there is danger if you
enter the woods.

Katerina Frantzanas (8)
Grange Park Primary School, Winchmore Hill

Animals

Animals have incredibly massive bodies like elephants standing up.
Every animal has vibrant, colourful skin because it can go in different colours.
Animals are waiting for their next prey.
Animals can sometimes be in a bad mood.
They can sometimes be vicious and sometimes attack.

Hasan Akarcay-Gungor (8)
Grange Park Primary School, Winchmore Hill

65 Million Years Ago

The mighty megalodon with its sharp menacing teeth,
Leaping about the wonderful waves,
As the red eye of the T-rex catches its gaze.

The dinocore approaches the water,
As silent as a mouse,
Suddenly, the megalodon snatches the dinocore in his mouth like a crocodile.

Abtin Abtin (8)
Grange Park Primary School, Winchmore Hill

The Puma

A savage scream hit the air
Rumbling away in the distance
She had a smell of a male puma approaching her
territory
She gave him a warning, a promise of what she would
do if he came any closer
She had three cubs behind her
And she would protect them with all her might.

Meryem Mercan (8)
Grange Park Primary School, Winchmore Hill

The Fire Dragon

D ragons hunting for prey,

R ed fiery eyes and fire coming out of its mouth,

A s big as a mountain,

G one like the Flash when you spot it,

O nce you challenge it you will regret it,

N ever fight the fierce, flaming, fire dragon.

Luca Murray (9)
Grange Park Primary School, Winchmore Hill

Animals

A wesome animals

N ever feed a tiger

I worked in a zoo

M ost people think animals are dangerous but some are not

A ntelopes are the tiger's prey

L ovely leopards leap at night

S erious koalas sleep nicely.

Aria Jangra (8) & Alexis

Grange Park Primary School, Winchmore Hill

Sub -0

S hivering more like a furless bear in the winter.

U nder weather also feeling the pressure.

B lowers blow hoo-ha, their hoot sounds like a balloon.

-

0 pieces of food and feeling dry, my tummy rumbles, it's like a hollow cry.

Zachary Osijo (8)
Grange Park Primary School, Winchmore Hill

What Am I?

I am as strong as a fierce lion.
I am as fast as a speedy cheetah.
I can swim as far as a silver shark.
I can climb as high as a legendary leopard.
I am as exciting as a black panther.
I have a beautiful pattern like a zebra.
I am a terrific tiger.

Malak Mahran (8)
Grange Park Primary School, Winchmore Hill

Golf

The ball with a smile.
The ball with two colours.
The ball with dimples.
The ball with a liquid centre.
The ball with mud on.
Golf is nice.
Only good on a summer day.
Lots of fun with every shot you hit.
Fill in the ball with divots.

Rian Mistry (8)
Grange Park Primary School, Winchmore Hill

What Is It?

It loves nuts.
The colour is reddish brown.
It always goes into hibernation.
It lives in a tree.
It climbs into a tree really fast.
It buries nuts into the ground and eats them later.
It makes a high-pitched scream.
It's a squirrel.

Selim Suleyman (8)
Grange Park Primary School, Winchmore Hill

My Culture

C ame from Lagos, Nigeria.

U nderneath Niger.

L ove my beautiful country.

T raditional dishes like shaki and semo.

U ltimate favourites.

R emember my country always.

E very day I wish I was there.

Zaida Hazzan (9)
Grange Park Primary School, Winchmore Hill

Trick Or Treat?

Knock, knock

You may tug and you may pull
But I'm not leaving till my bag is full
Just give me some sweets
Then I may leave
They finally answered trick or treat
Always pick treat
Who's there?

Me!

Ava Parsons (8)
Grange Park Primary School, Winchmore Hill

Italy

I t is very hot in Italy.
T he capital is Rome,
A s beautiful as a butterfly.
L arge mountains like Napoli.
Y ummy foods like pasta, pizza, very beautiful sea.

I was born in Italy, in Rome.
I love Italy.

Oliver Kola (8)
Grange Park Primary School, Winchmore Hill

Tigers

T igers roaring as loud as a drum,
I n the dark scary night, tigers run.
G rowling tigers having a feast,
E very young tiger becomes a beast.
R oars fill up the night sky,
S cary tigers begin to fight.

Nazanin Farhadi (8)
Grange Park Primary School, Winchmore Hill

Koala

K ind and as fluffy as a blanket,
O h no, quickly numbers are declining,
A n extraordinary sleep up to 18/20 hours,
L eathery nose and scrumptious eucalyptus,
A mazing Australia is their habitat.

Jasmine Shevket (8)
Grange Park Primary School, Winchmore Hill

Tiger

T he black strips on them are very delicate.
I can see that they are very loyal.
G ood and bad, I don't know how.
E ating and sleeping are all they do.
R oaring as loud as a drum.

Sayna Mofrad (8)

Grange Park Primary School, Winchmore Hill

Space

S pace is as dark as a black hole,
P luto is a blue bubbly ball,
A nd stars are bright like the sun,
C ircle planets blind my sight,
E very planet in the solar system catches my eye.

Libbie Angelides (9)

Grange Park Primary School, Winchmore Hill

Dinosaur Astronaut

Dinosaurs getting ready to launch into space with their space shuttle not scared at all. The little dinosaur gets out first and he says, "We are on the moon!" All the dinosaurs get out and they dance and sing and play.

Dimitri Karasas (9)

Grange Park Primary School, Winchmore Hill

The Wonders Of Christmas In Oxford Circus

In the night of Oxford
A day before Christmas
The streets are as busy as a mall.
As people walk by,
The lights twinkle brightly.
There, Christmas is a delight,
And there lies your Oxford night.

Ebrah Ali (9)
Grange Park Primary School, Winchmore Hill

Space

S tars in space, ready to race.
P eople struggling to breathe in space.
A steroids flying through the night sky.
C ool rockets zooming by.
E ach night I'm ready to fly.

Vincent Palmer (8)
Grange Park Primary School, Winchmore Hill

Litter

L ittering isn't good

I nterestingly, it includes food

T oxic waste kills

T errible trash

E ventually, people need to stop

R eally, this is not good.

Aaron Doondeea (8)

Grange Park Primary School, Winchmore Hill

What Is That?

What is that?

It is as big as an elephant.
It is as rare as a museum.
It is as colourful as a butterfly.

What is that?
I think it is a dragon,
A dragon about to eat you!

Alphan Selim Sener (9)
Grange Park Primary School, Winchmore Hill

Nature

Cheetahs running as fast as cars, never stopping,
Tall trees standing in the air.
Monkeys climbing like bars,
Monkeys never stop playing,
Lions running around, if they want they stop playing.

Kristian Koceku (8)
Grange Park Primary School, Winchmore Hill

Football

F antastic football
O degaard on the ball
O i oi
T hey chant
B alls flying across the sky
A mazing Arsenal
L ionel Messi is a legend
L aughing all the way

Leo Kyriacou (8)
Grange Park Primary School, Winchmore Hill

You'll Not See Anything Like The Harlequins!

From Danny Care to Marcus Smith,
Harlequins can win,
The Gallagher Premiership to the Champions Cup,
Maybe the treble!
And The Stoop? Glory it will bring!

Rory Megahey Townend (8)
Grange Park Primary School, Winchmore Hill

Immortal Creaking

The Creaking is immortal,
The Creaking can't drown,
The Creaking can't burn.

Don't mess with the Creaking,
Or you will regret it.

Atlas Ulgu (9)
Grange Park Primary School, Winchmore Hill

Christmas

The grassy green Christmas trees
Were as massive as a giant,
The sparkling silver baubles were as tiny as raindrops,
From out of the beautiful blue sky.

Lyra Codling (8)
Grange Park Primary School, Winchmore Hill

The Day Before Halloween

There is a wicked witch down the hallway
Meowing like a cat.
She turns into a cat;
It appears as a frog
Jumping in the hallway like a dancing cat.

Lilly Desai (8)
Grange Park Primary School, Winchmore Hill

The Robot

R eliable robot helps.
O n to a mysterious plan.
B *eep-boop.*
O pen-minded robot.
T iny robot in disguise.

Siyena Erboy (8)
Grange Park Primary School, Winchmore Hill

Ghost

G iggling gasps,
H aunted house,
O minous screams,
S neaky smoke,
T errifying nightmares.

Wynter Reyes (8)
Grange Park Primary School, Winchmore Hill

Best Friends

Respectful and kind,
Always on my mind.
Lots of playdates,
She's my best mate.

Ruby Rogers (8)
Grange Park Primary School, Winchmore Hill

Trick Or Treating

Dark gloomy night,
People are in for a fright.
Scary lights,
What a sight.

Hektor Kukeli (9) & Rafael Refahi (8)
Grange Park Primary School, Winchmore Hill

Volcano Voices

I am a volcano, I have a blazing heart,
Some people think I'm useless but I'm actually very smart.
I'll erupt when I'm angry and I'll burn what I can
And maybe I could catch a distracted man.

I'll burn nature's floor
With my rumbling flames until the people plead for no more.
I go boom! When I erupt, my crimson orange and scarlet red flames
Take revenge on those who call me names.

When I erupt my big black flames ascend into the atmosphere
With my uncontrolled sparks going here, there and everywhere
As my blazing fiery fire comes with intense boiling heat
As the people are frightened as I am a flamethrower that you can't defeat.

Tom Scott (11)
Lisnasharragh Primary School, Cregagh

Volcano Voices

I am a volcano.
With a flash of my fury, I erupt, and I roar.
I wear a crown made of ash and fire, my fiery bursts
are what I desire.
With my blazing blasts of fire, I make the earth swell.
I am like a big explosion from the sun.
With clouds of smoke, I blow off steam spitting out lava
like it is a dream.
With my explosions of fire, I go boom!
My fiery drops of crimson-coloured molten can burn
humans in seconds.
My massive craters are dents in the earth's floor.
People get nervous when they are near me because
they know if they get too close, they will get burned to
a crisp.

Kale Holland (11)
Lisnasharragh Primary School, Cregagh

Winter Land

In winter the ice is as cold as the North Pole,
The snow is as white as teeth,
The wind is singing a song like pop songs,
Ho, ho, ho, ho, Santa giving pretty presents but only if you are good.

The crunchy food is so good but if you are good you might choose what you are eating,
Cookies as crunchy as ice,
Magic milk ready for Santa,
The carrots are so good and you can taste the goodness.

The food is waking up ready to eat,
The cookie presents are amazing to eat,
You can do super snow angels in the snow,
You can do soft snowmen so nice.

Snowmen as cuddly as a teddy,
The snow is dripping on the floor,
The trees have no leaves on their branches,
The flowers are so pretty and cold in winter,
It is nice in winter.

Emily Morbey (8)
Seabridge Primary School, Clayton

Wonderful Winter!

In winter it's cold, windy and snowy, but it's magical,
The snow is as crunchy as crisps,
Outside in winter, it's as cold as a freezer,
The soft snow howls at night.
Bro, Bro, Bro.

The turkey dinner is tasty,
It's as tasty as cake.
The strudel with bright yellow custard,
It's delicious.
The custard is as bright yellow as the sun.
Santa gets warm magical milk and celebration cookies,
The cookies are as scrumptious as chocolate bars,
The cookies laugh at our Christmas jokes.
Yum, yum, yum.

La! La! La!
The joyful sounds of singing and laughing,
Makes me excited.
The Christmas carols are as loud as a rock concert,
Songs dance happily.
The slow songs are the best at Christmas.

Ho! Ho! Ho!
Santa gives many presents on his sleigh.

Jingle! Jingle! Jingle!
Santa has a coat and hat that are as red as a bright cherry,
His sleigh has golden swirls like shining stars.

Clatter! Clatter! Clatter!
The Christmas tree has bright lights over it,
The lights are as colourful as rainbows.
They can sometimes be crystal clear like diamonds.

Swish, swish, swish,
The hot chocolate is as hot as an oven,
The warm, misty, hot chocolate sways in the cup,
It talks gently to the air.

Oh, how I love winter!

Orlaith Rogers (9)
Seabridge Primary School, Clayton

The Magical Ride To Winter

Winter is a time when the world is at its most snowy.
Icicles hanging like chandeliers.
Brown frosty, frozen trees covered with snow.
Snow floating from the sky like tiny ballerinas.

Children twisting, gliding and twirling on the icy skates.
Friendly, frosty snowmen with gloves, hats and an
orange carrot.
Marshmallows bobbing in the hot chocolate warming
up the air.
Children dressing up in scarves and hats are cuddly
and warm.

Presents coming down the chimney with Santa and the
reindeer.
Christmas dinner cooking on the stove warm and hot.
Families pulling Christmas crackers open.
Santa's bag being dragged like a dress.
Santa's wrapping presents big and small.
Figgy pudding being eaten by children and parents.

Santa's red cloak dragging on the snowy floor.
The fireplace of oranges, reds and yellows warming
their toes.

Red holly grows on bushes and mistletoe hanging from trees.

Snow on the floor making boots wet and cold.
Red Chrismas hats with pompons and fluffy hats for sale
Happy children laughing to the music.
Christmas decorations cover houses in lights and snow.

Niamh Rogers (8)
Seabridge Primary School, Clayton

A Winter Wonderland

In a relaxing place, in a relaxing world with a winter wonderland right by your side.

Fire crackling, clicking and snapping but warm in your house
Watching the tree glow with baubles.

The weather as frosty as ice in the fog
Knocking down the snowman that I built because of the wind.

Turkey dinner, yum, yum in my tum
Crunch, crunch, crunch!
Cookies snap, sizzle and crinkle in the oven.
Turkey trees coming your way.

The New Year countdown 10, 9, 8, 7, 6, 5, 4, 3, 2,1 is stored in boxes waiting for you.
Christmas Day is here, presents open, open, open in the morning
Slide, crack, smack!
Presents as cool as a flamingo.
Family come round. "Hello, hi, welcome, come on in."
Family bring more presents
Scavenger hunts looking for presents.

Playing with your presents. "Oh yeah."
Christmas is amazing every year.

Winter is so cosy
It is as cosy as a bear
And is just lovely and beautiful.

Decorations are amazing in winter
You just can't believe how beautiful it is.

Emily Leech (9)
Seabridge Primary School, Clayton

Magical Winter

Winter is a time when it's at its most beautiful.
Freezing cold icicles falling from the snow-white trees.
When you go outside, the floor is like a big snowy
blanket on the floor.
Shimmering, twinkling icicles twirling on the trees up
above you.

Making snow angels in the diamond snow.
Drinking hot chocolate and wearing snug socks next to
the warm fire.
Going out looking for a big hill, making footprints
behind us and walking home.
Putting our feet in the fluffy snow like Mum, Dad, sister,
brother and dog, making a family.

Santa's bells jingling as he walks to the snowy white
door,
Cooking a big roast chicken ready for the family,
Wrapping lots of presents for them too!
Putting up the Christmas tree and the shining star on
top.
Sitting outside and looking up at the stars.
In the morning, we go out to play and throw snowballs
at each other.
Listening to children giggling and zooming down a big
hill.

When all the people are here, we go in and open presents.
After we eat some food and the big chicken we cooked.

Pollyanna Rushton (8)
Seabridge Primary School, Clayton

Wintry, White Winter

Winter is a time when the world is at its most bare.
Clear, crystallised icicles shimmering in the sun.
A soft, silky blanket of snow on the rooftop, falling like
a ballerina dancing in the air.
Tall, brown, bare trees overlooking the cream-coloured
snow covering the landscape.

Cheerful children drinking hot chocolate till the end of
Christmas.
Fathers going snowboarding at 20mph.
Swish, swash, sway!
Snowballs hitting snow sculptures, making snowmen as
targets.
Swish, crash, smash.
Scarves as itchy as a dog's fur that has never been
washed.

The footsteps of Santa on the roof.
Bang, bang, bang!
Reindeer flying through the clouds as fast as lightning.
Cheeky, cheerful children smiling as big as a banana.
The jingle of the bells on Santa's sleigh.
Children opening gifts to their hearts' content.
Lights flickering on the vibrant green trees.

Santa travelling side to side of the world.
Steamy chicken dinner with potatoes, mash, pigs in blankets and sprouts.

Cara O'Neill (8)

Seabridge Primary School, Clayton

Snowtacular Winter

Winter is a time when the world is at its most frosty.
Long, transparent icicles hanging, as cold as a freezer
like a traditional chandelier.
Trickling snowflakes dancing like a parachute landing
to the ground.
Bare, brown trees keeping their leaf population warm
inside.

Cheerful, charming children giggling merrily whilst
slipping down with their sledges.
Cosy, pleasant scarves covering soft necks.
Steaming hot chocolate like a campfire.
Snowballs flying dramatically in the air.

The scent of gleaming fires lit on colourful, traditional
diyas as beautiful as fireworks.
Children dressing up wearing glamorous crystal-like
clothes making rangolis with their mums.
Mums and dads dressing up gods in clothes and
cleaning up the house.
Flowers hanging from the doors like a garland.

Ananya Manjunatha (8)
Seabridge Primary School, Clayton

White Winter

Winter is a time when the world is at its most beautiful.
Shimmering icicles like a crystal.
Frosty, frozen snow covering the icy cold ground.
The brown trees standing on the frosty snow.

Cheerful, happy children laughing whilst sledging down
a snowy mountain.
Children having a snowball fight in the frosty snow as
parents call them in for a warm hot chocolate.

The loud footsteps of Santa's heavy boots.
Kids joyful as they can't wait till the next day.
Children's smiles as big as presents under the
Christmas tree.
Families going to celebrate Christmas.
Steaming roast dinner all warm and tasty in the oven.
Cheeky elves causing mischief.
Reindeer flying in the snowy air as Santa chills.

Charlie Allen (8)
Seabridge Primary School, Clayton

Wonderful Winter

Winter is a time when the world is at its most bare.
The snow like a white blanket covering the surface.
Chocolate brown trees with sharp icicles hanging from the branches.
Cold, soft snow gliding down from the sky.
Icicles like chandeliers in warm homes.

Cheerful, cuddly children throwing snowballs fiercely at each other.
Kids sledging down a tall hill.
Whoosh, swoosh, giggle!
Warm, furry foxes running through a white blanket in the forest.
Big, towering reindeer with antlers as big as skyscrapers.
Arctic foxes as white as snow.

Crunch, whoosh!
Owls as brown as big, bare trees.
Warm, furry owls hooting as loud as someone shouting in a megaphone.

Hashim Riaz (8)
Seabridge Primary School, Clayton

Winter Wonderland

The sky as foggy as a cave,
Thunder striking down like lightning,
Brhh, brhh.

Snow as crunchy as crisps,
Crunch, crinkle, crack.
Rain as light as a feather,
Snowman as colourful as a rainbow,
Drop, crinkle, crack.

Blankets as fluffy as a puppy,
Scarves as cosy as gloves,
Shiver, swoosh, whoosh.
Jackets as warm as a cloth,
Clothes like a brilliant sofa,
Swizzle, squash, squish.

New Year as fun as Christmas,
New Year as far away as Diwali,
Boom, crash, bang.
New Year like Diwali,
New Year like the Christmas celebration,
Swoosh, whoosh, crush.

Ryan Kumar (8)
Seabridge Primary School, Clayton

My Christmas

On a cold winter morning, the hail goes *tap, tap, tap* on the roof.
The snow is as white as clouds.
There's a yummy smell downstairs,
It's toast.

My family come round for dinner.
The chicken is giant.
We share thanks.
After, we go and play in the snow,
Crunch go my feet in the snow.
Flinging balls of snow,
Crash, it's a snowball fight
And then we snuggle on the sofa and watch some family films.
Hot chocolate, marshmallows and tasty, yummy treats.
Presents and a star for at the top,
Crackers for pulling and tasty crackling.

This is my Christmas, what is yours?

Esme Twigg (8)
Seabridge Primary School, Clayton

Winter Wonderland

Snow as soft as a cloud,
Hail as hard as a rock,
Rain as loud as an earthquake,
Ice as cold as a freezer,
Rain going *drip, drop, drip, drop,*
Hail like rocks.

Turkey as crispy as ice,
Cookies as crunchy as a biscuit,
Milk as cold as a fridge,
Hot chocolate as warm as an oven,
Turkey which is really juicy,
Cookies crunching, *crunch, crunch, crunch,*
Turkey screaming about to get eaten.

Elf on the Shelf peering at you,
Snow as fabulous as cotton candy,
Christmas trees as light as a fire,
Lights as bright as the sun,
Confetti, as shiny as silver.

Zachary Hopwood (9)
Seabridge Primary School, Clayton

Calming Winter

Winter is a time when the world is at its most
comforting
Small, red robins chirping in a frost-nipped tree
Snow like lumps of powdered sugar forming a white
abyss.

Small, smiling kids
Small, white snowballs around a field
Happy families snuggled up and warm
Tucked up in bed, on this magical eve
As the jolly fat man was about to arrive.

A blanket of darkness fell over the town,
As Santa arrived in his gold-trimmed sleigh
And shouted in the night, "It's that day!"
Jack Frost spreading snow over fields, forests and
lakes.
Chestnuts roasting on an open fire.

Ben Lowery (8)
Seabridge Primary School, Clayton

Snowy Winter

Winter is a time when the world is at its most snowy.
Smooth, shiny icicles on top of the icy cave and as cold
as a freezing freezer.
Cold, bare trees standing in the winter coldness.
Delicate, fluffy snowballs being thrown around
dangerously at each other.

Adults and kids sledding down hills,
Swish, zoom as fast as a car going 50mph.
Santa's bells ringing on Christmas night
And Santa delivering presents,
Wrapping and dropping them off at children's houses.

Hot Christmas roast dinners coming out of the oven,
Red, steaming hot dinners for everyone in the family.

Leo Saunders (8)
Seabridge Primary School, Clayton

All About Winter

Winter is a time when the world is at its most peaceful.
Small, cold snow falling from the sky like ballerinas.
Frosty, bare trees blowing in the wind.
Cold, winter breezes blowing in the day.

Warm, inviting hot chocolate steaming in the mug.
Playful, excited children playing in the snow.
Warm, toasty marshmallows toasting on the fire.

Christmas crackers banging with presents for the children.
Roasted potatoes crunching in the mouths of people.
The laugh of Santa putting presents under the trees.
Very happy children opening the presents.
Fast sledges zooming down a hill.

Benjamin Willday (9)
Seabridge Primary School, Clayton

Winter

Winter is a time when the world is at its most beautiful.
Icicles dancing in the sky like glistening diamonds.
Shimmering sky and frosty, frozen trees,
bare and brown, sparkling.

Cheerful children laughing happily,
whistling and slipping on the ice.
Snuggling with warm, delicious hot chocolate.

The children laughing happily getting their presents
under the Christmas trees. The bells jingling on the
trees and Santa saying, "Ho ho ho."

Children sitting, opening their presents.
The currants of the bread biscuits,
and figgy pudding melting on the open fire.

Oliver Taylor (8)
Seabridge Primary School, Clayton

All About The Frosty Winter

Winter is a time when the world is at its most chilly.
Shimmering icicles like a crystal.
Icy cold snowflakes falling from the sky slowly hitting
The warm cosy homes bouncing off the earth.

Cheerful, joyful children giggling happily
Whilst other children play snowball fights.
Warm, cosy scarves cuddling the floor.
Snowballs getting thrown at 100mph through the chilly air.
Whoosh, swish, bang!

Burning hot chocolate warming up icy fingers.
The jingle jangle of Santa's bells.
Excited children with smiles as gigantic as the sun heating the Earth.

Lincoln Messenger (8)
Seabridge Primary School, Clayton

Wondrous Winter

Winter is a time when the world is at its most snowy.
Simmering snow covering the land like a silky blanket.
Glimmering icicles hanging down from warm homes.
Bare, brown trees peacefully stood on the snow.

Snuggly scarves all silky and warm.
Families inviting people for hot chocolate and roasted marshmallows.
Cheerful children laughing whilst sledging and sliding.

The jingle of Santa's sleigh.
Joyful families with smiles as big as the sun as they decorate their trees.
Families ready to have hot, warm roast dinners.
Children hanging their stockings for Christmas Day.

Nia Koshy (8)
Seabridge Primary School, Clayton

Wonderful Winter

Winter is a time when the world is at its most white
Shimmering icicles like a diamond
Snow twirling off the roof gracefully falling to the ground
Cold, icy bare trees swaying in the wind.

Hot chocolate warming people's hands
Cheerful, cheeky children giggling happily whilst sledging down a hill
Snowballs flying dangerously at children's faces
Soft, scrunchy scarves warming people's necks.

Elves causing mischief in the dead of night
Happy children with smiles as big as an iPad
Warm figgy pudding crunching in people's mouths.

Theo Roe-Griffiths (8)
Seabridge Primary School, Clayton

What Is The Wonder Of The Year?

The wonder of the year, Christmas, when the frozen grass is like ice cubes,
Crunch, crunch,
Everyone likes to make a snowman or a snow angel,
They make it as fast as lightning coming down from the sky.

The wonder of the year, Christmas, when the animals make a feast and eat
Then they will sleep like they are in heaven for the rest of the month.

The wonder of the year, Christmas, when everyone has a feast with some turkey,
And some sausages and finally a huge piece of cake.
They all like to dance together and also sing like a pretty present.

David Kuruvilla (8)
Seabridge Primary School, Clayton

Winter Fun!

Snow as soft as a bunny,
Rain pattering on your driveway.
It's so much fun.
Frozen trees wave friendly,
And fog falls down, down, down,
Whoosh goes the cold winter wind.

Crunchy, crispy crisps,
Mm-mm, tasty turkey,
It's a food buffet.

Fire fun,
Crackle,
Warming our toes after playing in the snow.
Tired tales and robbing robins.

La, la, la, Christmastime is here, *hm, hm, hm, hm*.
December is fun for everyone.
Sledding and tobogganing are so much fun,
I love it.

Oliver Heath (9)
Seabridge Primary School, Clayton

Winter Land

Winter is a time when the world is at its most snowy.
The snow is as soft as a bear.
The weather, frosty as a fridge and trees covered with blankets of snow.

Joyful children grabbing snowballs, throwing them down hills dangerously.
Having fun whilst their parents make hot chocolate
And also snowboarding on snowy hills.

Jingle bells of Santa and elves always being cheeky and watching you.
Then you get presents on Christmas Eve, having so much fun
And warm hot chocolate on the table for you, warming your fingers for you.

Risu Kumar (8)
Seabridge Primary School, Clayton

Santa!

One night Santa will come to your house and give presents
And you will be surprised when you wake up.

Snow, snowballs
And snowflakes,
And friends like snowmen will be at the window.

You can touch snowflakes,
Once you touch one, you will look at one and it's as shiny as a diamond.
The snowflake is chilly, cold and hailing.

Santa rides his sleigh and you can hear his bells.
Ding, dong, ding.
Santa comes in your house and gives presents
And goes out of the house.
House after house.

Ethan Cole (8)
Seabridge Primary School, Clayton

Wintertime

Winter is a time when the world is at its most beautiful.
Clear frozen icicles shimmering.
Chocolate brown trees and colourful vibrant leaves,
Dancing from tree to tree.
Cheerful, joyful children
Sledding down a hill *whoosh, swoosh, sway.*
Snowballs flying through the air.
Warm hot chocolate.
Santa's belt jingling and reindeer eating carrots.
Family decorating the Christmas trees.
Opening presents together.
Chicken and potatoes, cauliflower and peas.
New fluffy pyjamas cuddling in a bed with teddies.

Flick Taylor (8)
Seabridge Primary School, Clayton

Winter Wonderland

The weather in winter is frosty, misty and foggy.
Snow as heavy as rocks.
Snowflakes shimmering.
Snow falling from heaven.

Christmas is a great time of winter.
Santa slowly delivering presents from the chimney.
Plop, dunk, whoosh.
Elf on the Shelf, as naughty as monkeys.

The food in winter is delicious.
Terrific turkey and carrot cake,
Coca-Cola and more.

Presents are the best things about winter,
Getting toys or teddies from friends or family,
Christmas cards as well.

Ronnie Abercrombie (8)
Seabridge Primary School, Clayton

Winter Weather

Snow as crunchy as crisps on a cold, frosty morning.
Hail as painful as falling down brick stairs.
Ice as weak as a balloon.
Stormy storms waving goodbye.
The icebergs are mountains.
Twinkle, crash, boom!

Presents as colourful as a Christmas tree.
Presents as exciting as New Year's Eve.
Presents as sweet as heaven.

Santa's beard, as white as snow.
Santa's bells, as loud as fireworks.
Santa's clothes, as red as a strawberry.
Twinkle, shuffle, shine!

Alfie Richards (8)
Seabridge Primary School, Clayton

The Season Of The Snow

Snow is a part of the winter.
Snow icicles drifting from house to house.
Snow as cold as the North Pole.
People building snowmen.
Ice cream cookie sandwiches, as tasty as sensational Oreos.
Ice cream sundae as sensatonal as Biscoff cookies.

In winter there are lots of activities
Such as amazing people building snowmen,
Accurate ice skating,
Active neighbours having snowball fights.
Plop, splash, crack, flop,
Exquisite cookies with steaming tea.
Apple pie waiting to be eaten.

Ahmad Ali (8)
Seabridge Primary School, Clayton

Winter

Christmas is like a ticking time bomb of presents and
no one can stop it.
When we go sledging it is as fun as a roller coaster
whizzing.
Tick, tweet, crack, click, crunch.
It is like you can taste the cookies and roast turkey.
I am excited, happy, thrilled, amazed,
You can smell the heavenly hot chocolate
And the cookies that crunch like fresh pie,
And the turkey is so tasty like a pack of sweets.
Sparks like little dancers,
Santa's bells going *clink, clack, ding.*

James Raby (8)
Seabridge Primary School, Clayton

Frosty Winter

Winter is a time when the world is at its most cold.
Glass windows frosting up in your house.
Joyful, happy children throwing snowballs at their friends.
Going snowboarding looking for the biggest hills.
Drinking hot chocolate to keep warm in winter.
The whipped cream tastes as nice as Pepsi Max.
Santa's bells jingling on Christmas Day.
Kids getting excited to open their presents that Santa has given them.
People celebrating their religions like Christmas, Eid and lots more.

Henry Vincent (8)
Seabridge Primary School, Clayton

Wonderful Winter Wonderland

Crazy hail running around,
Really rainy days sprinting around the country,
Silly snow as cold as a freezer,
Click! Clash! Whoosh!

Super Christmas dinner that I love,
Carrots as yummy as crisps,
Roast potatoes as lovely as a bar of chocolate,
Christmas pudding like a chocolate brownie.

Santa's beard as white as snow,
Whoosh! Click! Clash!
Santa's bells as loud as a lion's roar,
Santa delivering the waving presents.

Lucas Peart (9)
Seabridge Primary School, Clayton

Beautiful Winter

Winter is a time when the world is at its most beautiful.
Long clear icicles like razor-sharp knives.
Trees bare swaying gently side to side.
Cold soft snow gliding through the air.

Scarves as fluffy as dog fur.
Sledges skidding all over the place.
Snowballs flying viciously through the air.

The noise of Santa's sleigh landing on your roof.
Steaming hot emerald green Brussels sprouts.
Chocolate to be seen for miles and miles.

Max Bailey (8)
Seabridge Primary School, Clayton

Winter

Birds migrating *tweet, tweet,*
And mice hibernating in a warm hole.

Gooey marshmallows in hot chocolate by the kettle,
Warm gloves just for you.

Christmas cookies on a plate,
With Christmas dinner on the table ready.
Turkey as smoky as fire,
Crunchy potatoes in a bowl just for you.

Snowmen having snowball fights.
New Year's fireworks in front of your face,
Going *bang, crash, boom, poof!*

Lucas Raby (8)
Seabridge Primary School, Clayton

Winter

Snow as crunchy as crackers,
Frosty mornings not able to see anything,
Snowmen being built,
Rain days are coming,
Floods getting too much water and turning into a pool.

Roasting turkey and chicken in the oven,
Crispy yule puddings, *crunch, crunch, crunch,*
And don't forget the roast beef!

December is a time about super Santa with a
Christmas tree,
Awesome presents and wonderful toys,
And lots more!

Aryan Cheema (9)
Seabridge Primary School, Clayton

Frosty Forge

Winter is a time when the world is at its coldest.
White, crunchy snow, slowly diving down.
Frost over the floor, striking to the ground.
Windows frozen but slightly gleaming.
Clouds like fluffy, dark pillows hanging menacing in the white sky.

Hot chocolate making people happy and hopeful.
Soft scarves warming necks.
Children sledding down, down, down,
So much fun.
Sad, soft trees without their friend, leaves.

Annabelle Davies (8)
Seabridge Primary School, Clayton

Winter

Freezing like an ice cube,
Snow as white as wool,
Crunch goes the snow,
Dash goes the rabbit,
Flap goes the bird.

Birds as cold as ice,
Deer as small as trees,
Click, clock, click, clock go the horses' hooves,
Flap, flap, flap go the birds' wings,

Home as hot as fire,
Chocolate as good as heaven,
Socks as warm as Bonfire Night.

George Jones (9)
Seabridge Primary School, Clayton

Magical Winter

Winter is the most amazing time of the year.
Frosty, snowy, windy days with hail and rain.
Hail as cold as Antarctica.
Plop, splash, drip.

Yummy, delicious turkey.
Hot chocolate as warm as a jumper.
Slurp, munch, slurp.

Cosy, fluffy blankets as cosy as fluffy teddy bears.
Squash, squash, squish.
Snow as soft as a fluffy jumper.
Stomp, stomp, stomp.

Raghavi Kohileanthiran (8)
Seabridge Primary School, Clayton

Winter

Soft snow falling from the trees
Strong grass turned to soft snow
Girls and boys playing with the snow
Snow goes *slip, slip, slip*
Christmas trees everywhere
Snowflakes cold like a freezer
Snow is soft like a giant pillow
Presents everywhere
Everybody eating turkey for dinner. "Yummy"
Every child wants cookies, *crunch*
Children drinking hot chocolate, *slurp.*

Feyza Kose (8)
Seabridge Primary School, Clayton

Winter

The thunder is swirling in the foggy clouds.
The freezing snow, when stepped on, makes a crunch, crunch, crack.
The ice glitters, *glang, gling, bang.*
Santa comes and there are lots of presents.
Christmas is like a wonderful wonderland.
Opening presents is like a dream.
When you have hot chocolate, it tastes like a warm hug.
The turkey dinner is like a million dreams in one bite.

Wyatt Roberts (8)
Seabridge Primary School, Clayton

Winter

Snow as soft as a pillow.
The rain as loud as an earthquake.
Plop! Drip! Splosh!
Fog as gloomy as Halloween.

Christmas trees as beautiful as flowers.
Pretty presents for the puppy. *Woof!*
Elf on the Shelves, as naughty as thieves.

Hugging hot chocolate. Yum! Yum! Yum!
The crying turkey about to get eaten.
Crumbly cookies for Santa Claus. Ho! Ho! Ho!

Olivia Leech (8)
Seabridge Primary School, Clayton

Happy Holiday

No more sun, it's time for winter,
Whirling wind and snowy skies,
Magical sleet falling from the sky,
Smiles from a baby cousin, Ava,
And a huge dinner with family,
Munch, munch, munch.

Santa sneakily delivers presents to good children,
Tear off the paper and a surprise inside.

Christmas is fun but family is a big part of Christmas.

Annabel Johnson (8)
Seabridge Primary School, Clayton

Winter Wonders

Winter is a time when the world is at its most beautiful
The snow is like a cold silky blanket across the world
Cold silky snow flying through the air
Clear icicles hanging from window sills.

Cheerful, cheeky children laughing happily, sliding
On small soft scarves whilst running in the snow
Fluffy, furry foxes running through the snow.

Jude Mellenchip (8)
Seabridge Primary School, Clayton

Beautiful Winter

Winter is a time when the world is at its most frozen.
Shimmering, beautiful icicles hanging like diamonds.
The snow carefully coming down, dancing from the
roof.
The snow covering the bare brown trees.
Giggling children playfully rolling down snowy hills.
Snuggly scarves keeping everyone warm.
Snowballs flying dangerously through the air.

Alfie Dalgarno (8)
Seabridge Primary School, Clayton

Winter World

Snow as crunchy as crisps, crunch, crinkle,
Snowmen as cold as ice, *brr, brr.*

Ice skating on the ice skating rink,
Sledging down the slope,
Building snowmen,
All the fabulous fun,
Yay, woo.

Gloves as soft as a cloud,
Cosy pillows, blankets galore,

Always look on the bright side.

Alessi Collis (8)
Seabridge Primary School, Clayton

Winter

Winter is a time when the world is at its most beautiful.
The snow is dropping down gently onto the floor.
The frost is slippy and cold.
The shimmering icicles bounce a little when coming
down onto the floor.

We can sledge down a bank and have a hot white
chocolate.
Santa's reindeer like eating carrots.

Tyler Mclean (8)
Seabridge Primary School, Clayton

Winter

The snow is like candyfloss.
The ice is like slushies.
Fog is smoky.
The fireworks crackle.
Christmas trees glowing with baubles.
Snowmen wearing a Christmas hat.
Snowman cookies covered in icing.
Santa ate too many cookies.

Raees Mahmood (8)
Seabridge Primary School, Clayton

Christmas

Santa is as kind as Snow White.
The snow, as white as a white cat.
The baubles on the trees look like planets.
The fireworks, bright as the sun.
The snowman, cold as a freezer
Snowman feels happy
The snowball, as round as a rock.

Florence Green (8)
Seabridge Primary School, Clayton

The Day We Struck Gold

We were excited,
This would be a fun trip,
Unlike the museum,
Or a jog to the skip!

We went to an island,
Nearby our house,
We hoped to see rabbits,
Or maybe a grouse!

My parents agreed
And got the boat ready,
We set off with glee,
When they had held the boat steady.

We arrived at the island,
Jumping with joy,
Compared to the sea,
The size of a toy.

I tied up the boat,
With a tough sailor's knot,
I began to gloat,
Till my friends said: "What rot!"

We entered a cave,
Searching for treasure,
Maybe for glory,
Or maybe for pleasure.

Just as we
Were about to give up
With our last strike,
We struck with luck.

Truly an impressive haul
Treasure not for one,
But for all!

This was the day
That made us famous,
The treasure held by
Those infamous.

Pirates, plunderers and thieves,
Real people doing dastardly deeds.
Unlike those of noble steeds,
They needed this to suffice their needs.

We returned to our boat,
Appalled to find...

There was no boat
Onto which we would climb.

Ayanna Kirsop-Moran (10)
St Peter's Primary School, Bromyard

Stranded

Fuzzy. Blurry. Scorching sun. Where am I?
All I can remember. Heading back to the mainland.
Something happened. I'm overboard! Where is my bag?

Night. Darkness. Iridescent moon.
I searched the beach but all I found
Were coconuts, a penknife and a lot of rubbish.

Morning. Boiling sand. No shade.
Lapping water beneath my feet.
The morning was a non-stop sauna.
I found a dozen more coconuts
By the shoreline. But no water and no food.
When will help arrive?

Afternoon. Hot and famished.
I made friends with a gecko
And I found some sort of fruit.
I cut the fruit with the penknife
And I shared it with my new gecko friend.

Night. Silver slit moon. Help had arrived.
I started a fire and somebody saw it
And took me back to the mainland.
I was saved.

Emilia Jordan (11)
St Peter's Primary School, Bromyard

Stranded For The Last Time

A feeling emerged with the boat surrounding me,
Heartbreak across the deadly sea,
Pirates back at sea,
Aboard to find treasure,
Treasure nowhere near,
Boat hard as a rock,
My eyes meet a light,
A face I've met before,
Similar people,
Killer people,
Closer people,
I ran to freedom,
A boat I seek,
Time to find my crew,
Across the seven seas,
As the guards were chatting,
A boat,
My boat now,
I set sail,
I dashed around the cruel place at least five times,
Then I went to the pirates' part of the world,
Only because I'm the one and only Captain Jack
Sparrow,

I jumped to make my crew,
A nightmare to forget,
The sky didn't look good but now a storm crashed down,
I turned my head,
Then all of a sudden the ropes snapped,
The boat was floating away,
I dashed with my sweaty palms,
I reached out then... *boom!*
Darkness, murky and foggy.
I saw the ferocious, ravenous and killer waves over me,
Cold, freezing, and dangerous,
I was on the last of my luck,
I was in the ocean alone, all alone.

Mason Baker (10)
St Peter's Primary School, Bromyard

Alone On The Island

Hello
My name is Lucifer and I am on my flight to Korea,
It's my dream,
I'm so excited as a bird set free,
But my family is the opposite of me.

3 hours later,
I'm on my flight right now,
After waiting so long the flight started,
For 2 hours everything went all right,
But after that 2 hours the flight started to shake.
Bang!
Crash!

The flight crashed,
When I open my eyes to see what happened, the fear in my eyes is huge.
Because all the people are dead,
But somehow I'm alive,
I went outside to get some air and sat under a tree,
There is no food or water.

I'm starving to death,
After 7 hours,
The sky went black,

It means it's night,
There's a sound like *owww*,
I think it's a wolf,
I wish the rescue team would be here after knowing the flight has crashed,
After 11 days, the rescue team came to help me from that hell that looked like an island.

Delna Siby (11)
St Peter's Primary School, Bromyard

Where Am I?

I opened my eyes,
Blinded by the scorching sun,
I didn't recognise my surroundings.
Palm trees?
Sand?
Hot sun?
Where am I?

My boat on the island,
Surprised to be here.
I got up off the pale, yellow sand.

I looked up.
Grey clouds rolled in,
The storm is here.
Where am I?

I need shelter,
I need food,
I need water,
I need hope.
Hope to find shelter,
Hope to find home,
Hope, hope to survive.
Where am I?

Hours had passed,
Isolated on an island.
All alone...
Where am I?

Hours and hours passed,
Rain still pouring.
No food.
No water.
No hope.
Where am I?

The storm had passed,
Still no food,
Still no water,
Clear skies lit up the island.
Where am I?
Isolation took over my body.
It was lonely, very lonely.
I'm stranded...
Where am I?

Indie Mills (10)
St Peter's Primary School, Bromyard

The Missing Showjumper

A girl,
A girl on a boat,
A girl on a spectacular boat,
To the showjumping finals,
Her horse was onboard too,
Hours later she finally arrived,
Someone was getting her horse,
Suddenly he came running to her,
"Miss, Miss your horse has gone missing,"
The lady suddenly jumped up and sprinted to the boat,
She looked frantically from top to bottom of the boat,
She quickly spun the boat around,
Her words echoed, "My horse, my horse!"
She looked everywhere
Worrying that she could be in the water,
Hours had passed,
Sleepless hours had passed,
1am in the morning,
She suddenly heard neighing at her door,
She opened the door to be greeted by her horse,
Her horse looked pleased with himself,

He happily trotted to his stall and quickly put himself to bed,
She was shocked but grateful her horse had come back not hurt.

Poppy Eversham (11)
St Peter's Primary School, Bromyard

Stranded!

Washed up by the seas,
Where could I possibly be?
Blurry visions that make me barely see,
Armies of birds unite in song.
I regain my senses,
Realising the problem,
Will I get rescued?
Am I stranded on this island
All alone?
I began my search
A hunt for essentials.
I had to be cautious
Aware of the dangers lurking ahead.
It won't be long though
Till darkness awakens.
Scavenging for food and water
All I find is coconut and fruit.
That's two things down on my list.
Fire the most important
How do I make it?
I realised that if you use glass and leaves
Maybe, just maybe
I could light a fire.

Reflecting my glass at a good angle
(The glass that I found buried in the sand)
I waited.
After what felt like centuries later
I had a fire!
But I saw a shadow
What could that be?

Joshua Nhemwa (11)
St Peter's Primary School, Bromyard

Me And The Writing In The Sand

My eyes opened.
All I saw was a blur for a moment.
I stared at the infinite blue sky.
I stared until I could stare no more.
Where was I?

I sat up.
My head throbbing.
Realisation dawned on me.
I was stuck.
The vast, glimmering sea surrounding me,
Making me feel outnumbered.

I felt my stomach churn.
The sea was gentle,
But was it friendly?

The scorching sun's rays interrupted my thoughts,
Blinding me with its greatness.
Though, luckily,
The towering, tropical palm trees sheltered me.

But then I froze.
Big words spread across the sand.
The words were illegible,
Unreadable,
Unclear.

I wasn't alone,
Was I?
I yelled.
I screamed.
I screamed 'til my voice was pleading.

Ellie Evans (10)
St Peter's Primary School, Bromyard

Stranded On Storm Island

Washed up on an island by a monster of a wave,
The sky jet black,
Tornados, tsunamis, and splinters of wood
Overcast and ominous,
Nightmare black,
An angry wrath, deadly and dangerous.

The sea overlapping, my boat has crashed,
A seething rant, a rampage,
Pessimistic and petrifying,
A wave made horror,
The sea, the sky, my eternal enemies,
An army of flares, a terrorist of twisters.

Ebony, raven, murky, and grey,
Leven and ashen,
The raging weather,
Clouding and clawing,
I will never escape.

Whirlpools and lightning,
I am stuck here forever.
Darn thunderclap, I have tried my hardest,
The sombre rain reminds me of home,
I have met my doom.

Danella Major (10)
St Peter's Primary School, Bromyard

The Haunted Island

Stranded on a haunted island,
Ghosts creeping around,
Graves all around.
Creeping, cracking and creepy,
Is anyone here? I wondered.
I could see a haunted house in the distance,
Creepy sounds in the distance.
Things flying all around me,
Crack! I heard it again and again.

I think it's the house, I thought to myself,
Splinters of wood surrounded the haunted house.
Am I trapped here? I wondered.
Ghosts coming out of the graves.
Am I trapped in the haunted house?
I started to try to open the door to get out but I
couldn't!
What will I do!?
I didn't bring food.
Will I starve?
I will never know.

Olivia Mae (10)
St Peter's Primary School, Bromyard

Stranded!

Splash! Plop! Trickle!
She dived in,
The ominous sea,
Lurking for his next victim,

"Help!" screamed the sounds of the sea,
She had been washed up,
The twisted waves had wrapped around her finger,

I know you are wondering why,
She was on a boat,
The girl was on her way,
On her way to the Paris Olympics
Show jumping on her horse Apollo,

A few hours later,
She found herself,
Stranded on a beach,
The scorching hot sun burned her body,
The bright sun.

Her vision was blurry,
She was traumatised,
Beautiful but deadly.

She found a pen and a book,
Some water,
Some food,
She wasn't alone.

Bethany Cross (10)
St Peter's Primary School, Bromyard

Stranded On A Ghost Island

Wandering down its petrifying paths,
Ghosts sneaking up on you,
Waiting for the perfect moment to grab and terrify you,
A whoosh and a howl,
A bang and a shatter,
A scream and a boom,
A squeak and a natter,
The panther-black atmosphere was too dark to see
past my nose,
Grabbing my torch with my sweating palms,
What's lurking in the forest? Nobody knows,
Fog closing in on me, annihilating my senses,
The forest surrounded by prickly fences,
Tree trunks rotting,
Mysterious people plotting,
Search parties after me,
Crying and screaming,
Someone, please come and save me,
Nightmare black and blood red,
Someone, please find me before I drop dead.

Edie Meddins (11)
St Peter's Primary School, Bromyard

Stranded On An Island

S tranded on an island,

T roubles began,

R ising rays of sun beaming down.

A bandoned island, no life to be seen.

N o drinkable water or food.

D anger lurks in every corner.

E ndless water around the island.

D ark shadows swallow up the island.

O n an island all alone.

N othing to keep me company.

A ll hope is lost

N ow I'm desperate.

I call for help.

S oon the moon will rise.

L uck is on my side as I see a passing boat.

A ll hope has re-emerged.

N o one on the boat sees me.

D oom approaches.

Phoebe Phillips (10)

St Peter's Primary School, Bromyard

The Tale Of Coral Island

A man called Levi,
Twenty years old,
Walking home,
Everything was normal,
Until he arrived.
He opened the door
And was taken,
Transported far away,
The door shut,
No escape now.

After some time,
He found some resources,
Some wood and wool,
He had an idea,
Build a hut,
So he started to build.

After a while,
His base was complete,
But little did he know,
A new challenge would approach.

A creature soon came
And devoured the man.

Ever since that day,
People feared Coral Island,
Now no one dares to go,
Or even get close,
To Coral Island.

Alex Oakley (10)
St Peter's Primary School, Bromyard

Captured

A young girl who adores the sea,
Would venture into it like a bumblebee.
Clambering into her rowing boat,
Pulling around her shoulders, her coat

But one day some ebony clouds blanketed the sky,
But she carried on. Why?
She would give up? Never
Her willingness was as strong as leather

The storm hit,
The lightning bit,
She was thrown overboard!
She had nothing to grab not even a cord.

She washed up onto the beach of an island.
Lonely. Sad. Deserted.
Her boat was nowhere to be seen!

She suddenly heard rustling,
She was dragged into the dark forest,
She disappeared.
Where...?

Rebekah Perfect (10)
St Peter's Primary School, Bromyard

Away From War

Boom, clash, shatter.
Smoke fills the air.
People screaming at the top of their lungs.
My father I say is out, I don't know where.
My mother is working in the factories.
I get shoved on a large boat
Full of children.
I watch each one leave one by one.
It's only me left.
They threatened to take me back
But it's not safe.
Those cruel people ditched me
On an island.
How am I going to stay here?
I miss my parents.
I looked around.
Tears rolled down my cheek.
Coconuts, palm trees and sand.
Not much.
I need to make a plan.
But it's too late...

Albie Cartwright (10)
St Peter's Primary School, Bromyard

I Am Stranded On A Desert Island

The sun is blazing down like a dragon's eye.
The sun is so fiery like a dragon's breath.
I am lonely, I don't know what to do.
I am on a desert island.
Coconuts falling like rain.
I can hear the whistling of the colourful birds.
The navy blue waves crashed onto the beach.
I am on a desert island.
Searching for food.
I found a dog, I called her Luna.
Finally, we're together, nothing bad can happen to us.
The dog was bounding around happily because it found treats in my pocket.
Will Luna get lost?
Will our friendship end?
Are we going to find a home?

Julia Jaromin (10)
St Peter's Primary School, Bromyard

Stranded

A toss and a turn, the wave took me under,
It took me to shore with lightning and thunder.
My feet touched the sand
So hesitantly,
The sand was scorching
And the stones were cold.
Finally, I was out of the storm
With cuts, bruises and grazes.
The boat was eaten by the monstrous waves.
The storm drifted away
To ruin someone else's day.
A crunch and a rustle
From the leaves below my feet,
The darkness became light
And the island came to life.
The sun went away
And the moon took the light.
I could see nothing ahead of me
Nothing but darkness.

Theo Brittain (10)
St Peter's Primary School, Bromyard

On A Desert Island

On a desert island,
Coconut shells are stacked up like mountains,
Exotic plants grow up high,
Creating a mystical shelter.

The animals are squawking and talking,
Roaring and squeaking,
The waves are crashing and bashing against the rocky
shores.

I can see hairy brown coconuts and vivid orange
mangos,
Exotic red berries and purple flowers,
I can hear the blue crystal-like water and the green
grass swaying in the wind,
The pretty pink flamingos are dancing and prancing,
The bright yellow sun shines down on the island like
a lamp,
I can smell freedom.

Isabel Bilyard (11)
St Peter's Primary School, Bromyard

Stranded

Stranded,
Stranded but not alone.
Stranded but with someone I can trust.
We are living off crabs and coconut water.
We made a fire and had a feast but I felt like we were
not alone.
The next day we saw a message,
It said 'You are not alone'.
We hid on our hill petrified and terrified,
Later we found out who they were...
Cannibals
A tribe of cannibals.
We were found, we ran and ran and ran
Until we couldn't run.
Then we heard blades spinning.
A rescue helicopter.
We were saved.

Benjamin Taylor (10)
St Peter's Primary School, Bromyard

Takadea

Debris everywhere,
I stand, 127 don't,
Where were they?
Trapped and isolated,
Stranded.
Changing her identity and running away didn't help her,
They did this.
They are the reason it went down.
Parts of plane scattered,
One marked with a symbol,
Takadea.
He did it.
Slowly standing, slowly walking, slowly falling into tears.
Slow whispers fill her ears,
Eyes filled with cries,
Not knowing what's worse,
They had framed my father,
Or she has no communication to help.

Olivia-Rose Weaver (11)
St Peter's Primary School, Bromyard

Stranded!

Boom! Crash! Bang!
The plane has crashed,
I am stranded!
What do I do?

I see nothing but sand,
Hot, scorching sand.
After walking a bit, I found coconuts.
I also found the plane wreck,
There was a pocket knife in it.
I used it to open them,
The water is refreshing,
The coconuts are my source of food.

I also used it to make a spear out of a stick,
I caught some fish with it.
Before I could cook it and eat it, help arrived,
I am relieved to be back home.

Lucas Harper (10)
St Peter's Primary School, Bromyard

Stranded!

Alone on an island,
Is someone behind?
It feels haunting,
It has a deadly sound.

Closer and closer it gets to me,
Could it be the leaves of a palm tree
Or the lapping waters of the sea?

Darkness strikes and the sun drops down,
I was stranded on an island.
The sea goes silent,
The palm trees rustle.

The night went on,
A storm struck.
The waves twisted and turned,
The palm trees rustled and shook,
The lightning flashed,
The thunder crashed.

Jessica Maine (10)
St Peter's Primary School, Bromyard

Lost On A Desert Island

The palm trees swaying,
Splashing waves everywhere,
The sun burning,
I am on a desert island.

Whistling birds flying overhead,
Colours like sparkling gems,
I must be brave,
I am on a desert island.

I went to sleep and woke up,
A big turtle was by the sea,
It had a giant emerald-green shell,
I am stranded on a desert island.

I went over to get some air,
The big splashing waves,
Little green coconuts under the trees,
I don't know if I will escape here.

Amber Backhouse (10)
St Peter's Primary School, Bromyard

Stranded!

An elegant showjumper stranded,
With her majestic chestnut horse,
Stranded on a beautiful island,
With a small cottage,
Secrets hidden within the forest,
Its horses, majestic horses,
Riding her horse across the soft sandy beaches,
Jumping over a log in her way,
Flying,
Gliding,
Loving life,
Loving being alone with only her and her horse,
She, along with her majestic horse, galloped into the
unknown.

Esmae Greaves (10)
St Peter's Primary School, Bromyard

Stranded!

Stranded on the island, he went into the fog.
Sweaty palms, he was scared for his life.
With no help, no love.
He was almost fading away.
No food, no water, he was in the forest, scared.
All of a sudden a wild animal came from the bush.
Boom, crash, bang the animal went.
He was at the bottom of his life.
He saw the sea and the boat in bits.

Noel Marchant (10)
St Peter's Primary School, Bromyard

I'm On A Desert Island

The sun is hot.
The sun is like a tiger's eye.
The waves are splashing.
The waves are like dancing dolphins.

The sea is blue.
The sand is white.
The sun is yellow.
I'm on a desert island.

The sounds are quiet.
Where is my mum and dad?
Where am I?
Mum...? Dad...?
I'm on a desert island.

Isabella Pilliner (10)
St Peter's Primary School, Bromyard

Desert Island

It was hot.
The sun was a blazing dragon,
Coconut trees waved in the air,
I was on a desert island.

The sand was blazing like hot stones,
The sea was brilliant blue,
I was on a desert island.

The waves swaying up and down like a dancing
dolphin,
I was on a desert island.

Bright Mupedzi (11)
St Peter's Primary School, Bromyard

Stranded

The burning hot sun
Burns down like a dragon breathing.
I am on a desert island.

The sea splashing.
The waves dancing
In the hot sun.
I am on a desert island.

Where are my family?
What are they doing?
What do I do?
I am on a desert island.

Abhia Abhilash (10)
St Peter's Primary School, Bromyard

Stranded

I am on a desert island.
It is hot, my feet are burning.
I run off to get water.
There is no water.
What can I do?

I am on a desert island.
The sun looks like a dragon's eye
It is hot.
What can I do?

I am stranded
On the desert island.

Abigail Sabau (10)
St Peter's Primary School, Bromyard

The Life Of Harry Potter

There once was a boy named Harry,
Destined to be a star.
His parents were killed by Voldemort,
Who gave him a lightning scar.

Yo Harry, you're a wizard.
Harry goes to Hogwarts and meets Ron and Hermione.
McGonagall requires he play for Gryffindor,
Draco is a daddy's boy,
Quirrell becomes unemployed,
The Sorcerer's Stone is destroyed by Dumbledore.

Ron breaks his wand,
Now Ginny's gone and Harry's in mortal danger.
Tom Riddle hides his snake inside his gigantic secret
chamber.

Harry blows up Aunt Marge.
The dementors came and took charge.
Lupin is a wolf, the rat's a man
And now the prisoner is at large!

They used time-travel so they could save the Prisoner
of Azkaban,
Who just so happened...
To be Harry's godfather

(I don't really get it either)
Harry gets put in the Tri-Wizard tournament,
With dragons and mermaids
Oh no, Edward Cullen gets slayed!

Harry, Harry,
It's getting scary.
Voldemort's back revolutionary.
Dumbledore, Dumbledore,
Why is he ignoring your constant attempts to contact
him?

He is forced to leave the school,
Umbridge arrives,
Draco's a tool,
Kids broke into the Ministry,
Sirius Black is dead as can be, uh oh!

Split your soul,
Seven parts of a whole,
They're horcruxes, it's Dumbledore's end.

There once was a boy named Harry who constantly
conquered death
But in one final duel between good and bad
He may take his final breath.

Tilly Denton (10)
St Theresa's Catholic Primary School, Blacon

Jack And The Beanstalk

Once upon a time
There was a boy who lived with his mother.
They weren't rich
So they had to sell their items.
One day, the boy called Jack
Was walking around but then
An old man offered him three jellybeans for a cow!
Jack thought for a moment
Then he said yes.

The next morning,
A massive beanstalk was in his garden!
As he climbed
He was getting higher and higher...
He finally made it to the top
But what he saw next shocked him...
A giant! With lots of money.
He needed it so he took some but then it woke up.
Jack was so scared that he cut the beanstalk.
It turned to dust.

Daisy Andrews (9)
St Theresa's Catholic Primary School, Blacon

A Hunter's Heart

I prowl the world or just the floor,
My whiskers twitch as I seek for more.
Outdoors the wild cats call to me,
A life of freedom, bold and free.

The grass beneath my dinky paws.
The hunt begins.
I bring you gifts, I'm filled with joy.
A bird, a mouse, my proud display,
But your shouts chase my joy away.

Indoors, I watch from the window's ledge,
Soft and warm but bound by edge,
Yet still at night, the gifts I leave.
A hunter's heart though you may grieve.

Inside or out, I'm still the same,
Yours forever, now unchained.

Syra Howell (10)
St Theresa's Catholic Primary School, Blacon

A Portal To Another Universe

Once upon a time
A girl called Rosie
Was just about to get into bed
All of a sudden
She clicked a button on her glasses
Which took her to another universe
Another galaxy
Somewhere she had never been before
Mushroom groves, little gnomes
Running around, they looked like little puppies
Having an adventure just like Rosie!
But how does she get home?
Something just clicked in her head
Just click the button on your glasses
She clicked and Rosie was on her way home.

Daisy Partington (9)
St Theresa's Catholic Primary School, Blacon

The Amazing Super Ara/Tornado Boy

Super Ara was flying through the sky
Wondering what he could do
Today he saw a race
So, he flew down and hopped into his supercar,
But it became lighter than before
Oh no! It is Tornado Boy!
What should I do?
Super Ara pressed his super emergency button
And the car transformed into Super Ara MegaBot.
Cold froze.
For the win, I whoosh!
Say bye-bye, yeow!
Tornado Boy, defeated on the ground
You are too powerful, off to jail for you!

Araoluwa Ijasan (9)
St Theresa's Catholic Primary School, Blacon

The Lost Jungle Adventures

The lost jungle far away
Beautiful adventures, life today.
Creatures lurk in the distance
In burrows sleeping away.
Muddy footprints in the grass
Animals go fast
But sometimes they crash!
Sugar gliders glide away
But koalas sleep away.
Monkeys swing from tree to tree
But adventures also lay in the sea.

Rita Hughes (9)
St Theresa's Catholic Primary School, Blacon

The Beautiful Seasons

S un shines bright as night goes down
E ating waffles for breakfast
A s the stars go down, the sun comes up
S now is too cold, you can get frostbite!
O n the mountain, the climbers were very proud
N ew Year, new personalities
S un is so bright, it's blinding.

Crimson Harris (10)
St Theresa's Catholic Primary School, Blacon

Emotions On Your First Day

E xcited to get there

M isunderstood by other children

O verjoyed to play

T ired waking up this morning

I nterested to learn more

O verwhelmed with everything new

N ervous about what is going to happen

Emotions - everyone has them!

Kaiden Hampshire (9)

St Theresa's Catholic Primary School, Blacon

A Day In Rhyming Space

One day on a space base
I was running a race
With my friend after I packed my suitcase.
My friend gazed at my face
Whilst he ate an apple.
Then I tied my lace.
I went to Mars
And I made a car.
And when we went home
I made a trace.

Alain Kamtchouang (9)
St Theresa's Catholic Primary School, Blacon

One Day In Space...

I was making a cake in a base.
In space, I was running a race.
In space, I was sleeping in a base.
On Mars, I was making a bar.
In space, I was making a base.
In space, I was in a case trying to tie my lace.
In space, I was dancing on a base.

Jacob Andrews (9)
St Theresa's Catholic Primary School, Blacon

Cinderella

C arriage
I magination
N aughty stepsisters
D isney princess
E nchanted
R ing
E vil stepmum
L ove
L ikeness
A baby blue dress.

Poppy Barnett (9)
St Theresa's Catholic Primary School, Blacon

The Amazing Galaxy

Portal through the sky
In this world
There is a portal in the sky
When you go through it
It's a wonderland!
It's a rainbow through magic glasses
Bright purple stars
An amazing galaxy.

Cara Connally (10)
St Theresa's Catholic Primary School, Blacon

Superheroes

Superheroes are people who save the world
Superheroes protect the city
Superheroes help people
Superheroes are lifesavers
Superheroes have superpowers
Superheroes take action!

Jeffery Ogedegbe (9)
St Theresa's Catholic Primary School, Blacon

On The Red Bed

On the red bed,
Fred and Ted jumping on their red bed,
Dad shouted, "Get off the bed!"
They said no,
So out the window, Ted will go.

Jake Mapp (9)
St Theresa's Catholic Primary School, Blacon

YOUNG WRITERS INFORMATION

We hope you have enjoyed reading this book – and that you will continue to in the coming years.

If you're the parent or family member of an enthusiastic poet or story writer, do visit our website **www.youngwriters.co.uk/subscribe** and sign up to receive news, competitions, writing challenges and tips, activities and much, much more! There's lots to keep budding writers motivated!

If you would like to order further copies of this book, or any of our other titles, then please give us a call or order via your online account.

Young Writers
Remus House
Coltsfoot Drive
Peterborough
PE2 9BF
(01733) 890066
info@youngwriters.co.uk

Join in the conversation!
Tips, news, giveaways and much more!

f **YoungWritersUK**   X **YoungWritersCW**

📷 **youngwriterscw**   ♪ **youngwriterscw**